Business Bogging

B. Vincent

Published by RWG Publishing, 2021.

While every precaution has been taken in the preparation of this book, the publisher assumes no responsibility for errors or omissions, or for damages resulting from the use of the information contained herein.

BUSINESS BOGGING

First edition. June 16, 2021.

Written by B. Vincent.

Also by B. Vincent

Bridge Pages
Business Acquisition
Business Bogging
Marketing Automation

Table of Contents

Business Bogging

H ello, and welcome to this course on Blogging. In this course, we're going to cover how to leverage a blog for your business. This course is divided into three modules, *Module 1* gives us a quick overview of blogging, *Module 2* goes over various places or platforms where you can blog and *Module 3* covers a variety of topics you can treat with your blog posts. By the time this course is over, you'll know how to effectively leverage blogging and content creation for your business, so without further ado, let's dive into the first module. Okay guys, welcome to Module 1, in this module, our expert will give us a general overview of blogging, so get ready to take some notes and let's jump right in.

Module 1

Lesson one, <u>introduction to blogging</u>. Blogging is the process of sharing information on your website, usually in a reverse chronological order where the latest posts appear first at the top. A blog is the most effective way to reach out to your current customers and attract potential ones. In lesson one of this course, we'll dive into how blogging can boost your business, where to find resources and how to choose the right blog content to feature. In lesson two, we'll have a brief overview of the different platform options for blogging, the importance of frequency and posting content and the best mediums for your content to reach an audience. Finally, lesson three will guide you in coming up with content ideas, creating and following a schedule and how to monetize your blog. Whether you're thinking of starting a blog or improving an existing one, this course will highlight the fundamentals of all things blogging.

What's the most important tool for increasing brand awareness? For successful businesses, they all resound with one answer, "blogs". If your business doesn't have a blog yet, then you're missing out. Blogging is the most extensive channel for business visibility, customer interaction and increased profitability. Here are a few statistics that can back that up. Company websites that have blogs have 55% more visitors, 97% more inbound links and 434% more index pages. There are more than 500 million blogs in 2020 making up one third of the whole internet. 61% have purchased the product from a blog recommendation. Marketers who make blogging a priority are 13 times more likely to achieve a positive ROI. Whether you're a startup company or an already established business, having a blog is an excellent resource to elevate your business to the next level. Time is needed to build credibility and an audience, so setting up a blog should be done ASAP. Blogs are a gateway to connect you to your target audience, they boost traffic, making you visible to more people and create quality leads to your website. Moreover, a well-established blog strengthens your brand's voice, giving you an edge among competitors. Blogs are highly accessible and customizable, so you can tailor the one that perfectly suits your business's needs and preferences.

By utilizing your blog, you can create relevant and up-to-date content that will help build your reputation as an industry thought leader. It's always important to remember that blogging is not something you need to figure out on your own. In fact, most of the blog content you see today, didn't derive from an entirely original concept. With the vast number of blogs that were already established, many have used this as a medium to draw inspiration from when creating their own content. However, there's a big difference between inspiration and plagiarism. Instead of copying content word for word, you can build your own voice by learning from the writing style and structure of others and use these as building blocks for creating your own identity. Then you make it your own by injecting your new ideas into your fundamentals. To find inspiration, you get a habit to browse other businesses' blogs to see how they build and preserve their content. This helps widen your perspective of blogging and in time will help you understand the do's and don'ts of creating content. The best way to find resources is by understanding what exactly you're looking for. If you're looking at how to develop your own voice, search for leading business blogs, if you want to analyze the most popular blogs in your niche search for industry leaders. If you're looking to brainstorm new ideas to stay ahead of the competition, take a look at your competitors' blogs. Soon you'll have a compilation of blogs that you can read and use for drawing inspiration and creating your own content.

Starting a blog can be challenging at first, there's a constant dilemma of what topics you should and shouldn't write about, how wide or narrow the scope be, and most importantly, how would you form your own identity? Sadly, a common mistake that business owners make is creating a blog based on their product. However, for your blog to attract potential customers, it should be based according to their needs and not the other way around. This is why analyzing your target audience is essential for creating your blog's structure. Take a look at your target audience, what kind of blogs are they reading? Are they looking for product recommendations? Are they always on the look for the current trends in your industry? If you can identify what your audience reads, it will be easier for you to decide what kind of content will drive traffic to your site. There are a lot of helpful tools that you can use to identify what kind of topics do well in your niche. Tools like Ubersuggest, BuzzSumo, SEMrush, and Alltop, help you to analyze the most popular and shared contents of your competitors.

Module 2

Hey folks, welcome to Module 2. In this module, our expert will go over various platforms or places where you can blog, so get ready to take some notes, and let's jump right in.

Lesson two, <u>where to blog.</u> It can be difficult to decide where to post your blog when there are tons of options to choose from. In this chapter, we'll go through some of the best and most popular blogging platforms available. Your website, this is a no brainer, if your company already has a website, the best place to have your blog will be alongside the rest of your content. However, not all websites are built from scratch, some company sites are built using website builders and blogging platforms, which will be the structure of our following options.

Wordpress.org, wordpress.org is the world's most popular blogging platform. To date, there are 455 million websites built through WordPress, making up to 35% of all websites in the world. It's known for being incredibly customizable, allowing you to insert a lot of add on features like forums, online stores and membership options.

WordPress is the number one choice of most people to build their own website. If you plan to grow your blog into a full website, this is your best option. Another well-known feature of WordPress is having the luxury of choosing from thousands of free themes and plugins. Plugins are basically apps that extend the functionality of your website, enabling you to add more features like contact forms, galleries, timelines, et cetera. These powerful tools make the most out of your site, turning it into a more elegant, yet accessible page, however, don't confuse wordpress.org with wordpress.com, there is a difference. The main distinction between the two is that wordpress.org is a self-hosted solution, meaning that it requires you to provide a hosting provider. This is a great option as your goal is to have full control over your blog. On the other hand, wordpress.com takes care of the hosting for you and it's best suited for hobby bloggers and family blogs. However, the features and options are very limited compared to wordpress.org, so when creating a blog for your business, make sure that you're signing up on wordpress.org and not wordpress.com.

Wix, like WordPress, Wix is very easy to use even without any programming experience. With its signature drag and drop tools, you can design your very own blog in just a couple of minutes. These stools take away the rigorous part of building a website; the coding. In fact, Wix is mainly intended for users who want to build a website without any coding experience, however, its free account has quite limited options like third-party apps support. Using the free version also means that it will display the Wix watermark as well as its own ads on your site. Another downside is that you can't change your theme once you've chosen a template. If you want full access to all of Wix features, you need to avail their paid plans, starting from 12.50 to $24 a month. Note however that even its paid features like e-commerce tools are limited compared to big platforms like wordpress.org.

Blogger, Blogger is a free blog publishing service owned by Google. It's user-friendly and suitable for those who want to start a blog without any technical skills. More importantly, it takes advantage of Google's robust security and reliability. It's highly accessible, having an interface similar to Google plus profile and an editor looking like a docs page. Blogger is a solid solution for personal blogs, but may not be the best option for business purposes. It has very limited design options and third-party apps are below par. Moreover, probably its biggest drawback is being limited to basic blogging tools, making it incapable of expanding to a full website once your business grows. Another disadvantage is that Blogger has a history of canceling projects without warning; this means that Google can suspend your blog at any time.

Squarespace, Squarespace is a paid platform that's user-friendly and has a great range of professional website templates that are well optimized for phones and tablets, and can be customized to your preference. Squarespace is a great option for bloggers and contains features for blogs like commenting features, multi-author functionality, post scheduling, and more. Another aspect that makes Squarespace stand out amongst competitors is its editor usability. With its new feature, you can now edit content in real time, without switching back and forth between the site manager and preview mode. With Squarespace's online editing, you can now edit faster and easier, however, they're not allowed to features and third-party integration options available. It also has limited SEO customization, which limits your blog from becoming SEO friendly. Their personal plan starts at $12 a month, while their business plan starts at $18 a month. However, if you plan to keep your expenses at the minimum, while still taking the full advantages, you may want to switch to a different platform like WordPress.

Weebly, Weebly is a website and e-commerce service very similar to Wix, and it can be said to be close rivals. Like Wix, Weebly is based around drag and drop components, making it easy to build a website in no time. It has customizable layouts and a bunch of free themes to choose from, however, it has limited blogging tools and you need to pay more to get better customer support. Their paid plans include a pro account for $12 a month and a business account for $25 a month. They have a connect account for $5 a month that just basically allows you to connect a domain, so it's not worth paying for. Once you've chosen your platform and finished setting up your blog, the next thing you need to do is consider how often you should post content. A simple answer is this, it depends on what's best for your company. However, let's take a look at some statistics to see how many posts businesses found to have more success.

Blogs that post two to four times per week, get the biggest traffic, companies that publish 16 or more blog posts per month, get almost three and a half times more traffic than those who post four or fewer times a month. In companies of every size, posting 11 or more blog posts a month created at least double the traffic of those who rarely posted. The lesson, *'The more consistent your posts are, the better.'* When you have a regular frequency of blog posts, you increase your organic traffic or referring to the visitors that land on your website. More importantly, regular content increases brand awareness, giving you credibility as a trustworthy source of information for your target audience. For your blogs to reach the highest number of people, you have to use all the channels available for sharing content, this can be in the form of social media, email lists and paid searches. The beauty of having blog content is that it can be easily shared with your existing social media accounts, as well as your email lists. When you share your content with your existing audience, there's a good chance that they will help you spread the word by sharing it with their own platforms. When creating content make sure that it's integrated with search engine optimization or SEO.

SEO is the process of improving the quantity and quality of traffic to your website, so you can rank higher in search engines. You must ensure that every blog is SEO optimized so you can get the most traffic out of it. To make your blog SEO friendly, you need to be able to apply on-page and off-page SEO. On-page SEO refers to optimizing web content in order to rank higher in search engines. These techniques include optimizing title tags using focus keywords, mobile optimization, and more. On the other hand, off-page SEO focuses on increasing the authority of your domain by getting links from other websites. This includes backlinks, social media marketing, guest blogging, brand mentions, and more. When your blogs are SEO optimized, you'll rank higher in search engines, increasing your visibility to potential customers. The best content for search engines is information that provides solutions to questions asked by customers. When your content is built in a way that you answer specific questions in mind, the more likely that potential customer will read your blog.

Module 3

All right, welcome to Module 3. In this module, our expert will cover a range of topics that you can write about in your blog, so get ready to take some notes and let's jump right in.

Lesson 3, <u>Blog topics.</u> Coming up with blog ideas can be daunting, especially if you're not used to creating content on a regular basis. However, once your content starts to grow, you can recycle your old content by expanding the subject more or injecting new and up-to-date information. Here are some post ideas that can help you get started. Current trends or news in your industry, interview an expert or leader, listicles, pros and cons, points out common mistakes that users make, how-to tutorial posts, write a series. Guest posts from industry leaders, guides to buying the right product, answer frequently asked questions, beginner's guides for products, comparison of similar products, feature a customer success story. The big advantage of having these blog ideas is that it can be built upon one another. For example, a post answering frequently asked questions shared on social media will invite more questions in the comments. When you have enough questions, you can create a second post. Remember that the key to attracting customers is by creating interactions. Customers love to engage in content that relates to them, so make sure that you're creating engaging content by involving them. A good example is by asking them a specific question at the end of each blog and encouraging them to share their thoughts. Blogging can be pretty intensive, especially if you plan to post several times a week. Fortunately, there are a lot of organizational tools to keep you organized, and so you can strictly follow your content calendar.

Tools like Trello, Asana, as well as scheduling tools like Sprout Social and CoSchedule help you to keep on track and stay on schedule. The duration for creating content really depends on the person who's writing, for some, they prefer to write their posts one at a time, according to their posting schedule. Others however, prefer to dedicate one to two days a month to write blogs in bulk, so that they can publish posts from their cache. Sadly, some business owners feel that they have too much on their plate and simply don't have the time to create a blog. This results in some businesses not making a blog at all, however, don't make this an excuse to miss out on such a powerful resource. If you don't have the time to blog yourself, consider outsourcing to a freelance writer, they possess the right writing skills, as well as the time dedicated to creating content on a high standard. There are a lot of freelancing platforms where you can find the right writer for you, and if a long-term relationship is established, you can get all of your content done without having to hire a new person every time.

Many companies have utilized outsourcing and have proven to produce great results. It's no secret that a lot of companies make the most out of their blogs by monetizing them. The most common way to earn money from your blog is by displaying ads on your site, you can earn by the number of views or clicks it receives, this generally works best for high-traffic sites that have thousands of visitors each day. However, it's important to consider how the ads should be displayed as it might affect your reader's enjoyment and reading time. A more subtle approach to earning money is by the use of affiliate links. You use affiliate links to endorse brands that are relevant to your industry and that you personally recommend using. To create your own affiliate link, you have to reach out to a company and join their partner program if available. Once you applied for the program, they will provide you with a unique link ID that you include in your blog posts. When a reader clicks this link and buys the product, you receive a commission. Like ads, affiliate links work best for large blogs, so this might be something to put on hold right now. However, don't refrain from using it, especially when you're writing posts about specific products. Blogging can be time consuming and demands creativity as you constantly think of ways to reach your customers. This might seem to be a stumbling block for others, but once you've got through the learning curve, you'll surely reap the rewards of blogging. Consistent content can double or even triple your website traffic and will help establish your brand voice that customers can trust. So what are you waiting for? Start blogging today.

Don't miss out!

Visit the website below and you can sign up to receive emails whenever B. Vincent publishes a new book. There's no charge and no obligation.

https://books2read.com/r/B-A-QWUO-ZGPPB

BOOKS 2 READ

Connecting independent readers to independent writers.

Also by B. Vincent

Bridge Pages
Business Acquisition
Business Bogging
Marketing Automation

About the Publisher

Accepting manuscripts in the most categories. We love to help people get their words available to the world.

Revival Waves of Glory focus is to provide more options to be published. We do traditional paperbacks, hardcovers, audio books and ebooks all over the world. A traditional royalty-based publisher that offers self-publishing options, Revival Waves provides a very author friendly and transparent publishing process, with President Bill Vincent involved in the full process of your book. Send us your manuscript and we will contact you as soon as possible.

Contact: Bill Vincent at rwgpublishing@yahoo.com www.rwgpublishing.com

www.ingramcontent.com/pod-product-compliance
Lightning Source LLC
Chambersburg PA
CBHW030536210326
41597CB00014B/1179